Lewis & Clark Country

Lewis & Clark Country

"The object of your mission is to explore the Missouri river, & such principal stream of it, as, by it's course communication with the waters of the Pacific Ocean, may offer the most direct & practicable water communication across this continent, for the purposes of commerce." (Jefferson's instructions to Lewis, June 20, 1803)

Photography by David Muench

Text by Archie Satterfield

ISBN 0-915796-12-0
Library of Congress Card Catalog Number 78-8324

(Cover) Sunrise at confluence of Snake and Columbia Rivers, Sacajawea State Park, Pasco, Washington
(Preceeding page) Jefferson River at Three Forks, Montana
(Facing Page) Autumn flow: Eldorado Creek in the Bitterroot Range west of Kamiah, Idaho

Publisher: Robert D. Shangle
Company: Beautiful America Publishing Company
        202 Northwest 21st Avenue
        Portland, Oregon 97209
Designer: Bonnie Muench

Contents:

Sunset on Snake River near Pasco, Washington

Prologue

Just as the events of 1776 pushed Western civilization's conception of justice and human dignity into uncharted territory, the Lewis and Clark Expedition of 1804-06 gave physical shape to our new nation by stretching our geographical boundaries to the westward limit. If the Declaration of Independence was an experiment in idealism, the expedition was an exercise in pure exploration. Unlike European explorers who spent almost equal amounts of time murdering local residents and claiming the land they found for church and crown, Lewis and Clark returned with knowledge in their journals instead of wealth in their pockets.

It is significant that both the Declaration of Independence and the expedition resulted from practical dreams by practical men, such as Thomas Jefferson. We will never know, of course, but one suspects the expedition would never have occurred, or yielded so much information, had a president other than Jefferson sponsored it and men other than Lewis and Clark led it. But the time and circumstances were perfect for the orders of Jefferson and the selection of the leaders to carry them out. Their devotion to duty without complaining, without excuses for failure, make them equal partners with Jefferson in creating a new nation out of the wilderness.

There was only one flaw in Jefferson's overall plan for the expedition; he did not reserve a space on the journey for an artist, and it wasn't until three long decades afterward that a talented artist, George Catlin, did retrace much of their route. But by then the culture of the Indian tribes along the Missouri River already was in a state of flux and Catlin's art only approximated what Lewis and Clark saw.

Today the route is totally changed most of the way from the St. Louis vicinity to Astoria, Oregon, but with this book it is much easier to visualize the trail. You will find virtually no trace of man's alteration of nature in this collection of photographs, a difficult task one can appreciate only by retracing the route with a camera or an easel. A chain of dams on the Missouri River, utility poles and lines, freeways, dikes, cities, farms, land-clearing projects, bridges — all have taken their toll on the landscape. More of the same is inevitable unless plans to create a national parkway along their route are successful.

But when President Jefferson sent out the expedition to the Pacific, the nation west of the Mississippi River was total wilderness in the white man's definition of the word. True, the Spanish were lodged in the Southwest from New Mexico to California but what lay north of Texas to the Arctic and westward to the Pacific was only a matter of conjecture. Some trappers had followed the Missouri River north into the Dakotas, and perhaps had ventured a bit west on the Yellowstone River, but what is now Montana, Wyoming, Colorado, Utah, Idaho, Nevada, Oregon, and Washington were unknown areas. There were whole mountain ranges, wide rivers, and long valleys — and peoples — no white man had seen.

Jefferson wanted this land, whatever its value, for America, and he hoped an expedition would be successful in finding an all-water route across the wilderness with only a minor portage between the Missouri and Columbia River systems. Since it would be wasteful, and something to be regretted later, to send explorers all that distance for only one reason, Jefferson presented them with a remarkable set of orders, perhaps the most comprehensive and humane orders ever given explorers.

They were ordered to study and collect samples of the flora and fauna, and took instructions in taxidermy and flower-pressing; they were ordered to make celestial observations at regular intervals; to describe the landscape around them, keeping an eye out for mineral potential; to draw up vocabularies of Indian tribes they visited, in addition to writing anthropological reports while living in peace among them . . . the list went on and on, and it is no wonder that the explorers' notebooks ran into the hundreds of pages. The orders were so sweeping, yet detailed, and the explorers' reports so voluminous that some scholars have made Lewis and Clark lifetime careers.

There was stiff competition between Spain, France, England, and the new American nation for the land to the west, and the British, through the Hudson's Bay Company, held a strong claim to the part of the continent Lewis and Clark would go through. But Jefferson, no amateur in power diplomacy, pulled off a diplomatic coup that swung the power his way. Napoleon's government, strapped for cash, sold France's Louisiana Territory to the United States for $15 million while the Lewis and Clark Expedition was still in its embryonic stage. The Louisiana Purchase consisted of the entire Mississippi drainage westward to the Continental Divide, and north to about the present border of Canada.

With this purchase the explorers would at least be covering their own land much of the way, and added a new duty to their mission: that of convincing the Indian tribes along the route that they had a new Great White Father (when many neither knew nor cared that they already had one) and that they should pay homage to the new government.

Jefferson hired Meriwether Lewis as his personal secretary, with the aim of training Lewis as his mind and eyes on an expedition to the Pacific. Lewis was trained in many of the natural sciences and educated in what little was known about the Indians of the West. Jefferson selected him because they were old family friends in Albemarle County, Virginia, and Lewis had served well in the 1794 Whiskey Rebellion in Pennsylvania. By 1799 he was 26 and a captain in the 1st Infantry Regiment.

Jefferson permitted Lewis the choice of a co-leader, and without hesitation he chose William Clark, an old friend and former soldier who had served under General "Mad Anthony" Wayne in Indiana and Ohio, learning engineering, military construction, and cartography as well as something about Indian culture when he wasn't fighting them. (He won the few skirmishes he had with them.) When Lewis wrote Clark making the offer, he took no chances and asked another friend, Moses Hooke, to be his backup choice, but Clark was anxious to go and it became the Lewis and Clark rather than the Lewis and Hooke Expedition.

Lewis spent a frustrating spring and summer during 1803 trying to get the expedition under way from Pittsburgh, where he was having a keelboat constructed by a hard-drinking boatbuilder. He wanted to get started down the Ohio River before the low water of autumn, but the boatbuilder and other delays kept him there until late September. Finally, with a crew of recruits, few of whom lasted the entire expedition, he set out drifting the Ohio and hiring farmers to bring their teams of horses down to the river and pull the keelboat off the multitude of sandbars they struck.

Lewis apparently hired and fired recruits frequently along the route, and so far as is known, hired only two permanent members of the expedition: John Colter, who caused them a bit of trouble in the early going but settled down to become a valuable member of the party, and later was famous as a trapper and the discoverer of what became Yellowstone National Park; and George Shannon, the youngest member of the expedition who showed a remarkable talent for getting himself or his belongings lost throughout the expedition. Sometime during the first weeks of the expedition, Lewis also acquired a big Newfoundland dog named Scannon, who went to the Pacific with them, and at least part of the way back. Since the journals make no mention of the dog during the last stages of the journey, we can only assume he returned. By that time he was such a familiar part of the group that we can almost be certain he would have received some mention, if not a formal funeral, had he passed on to his reward.

Lewis and Clark finally met at Clarksville, Indiana Territory, on October 15, 1803, and Clark had several recruits with him waiting for the keelboat. He also had a slave (servant, in the polite terminology of the time) named York, who would accompany them to the Pacific and back. After a brief stopover there and at various other villages and posts along the Ohio, the small group drifted on down to the mouth of the Ohio, then poled and sailed up the Mississippi to a campsite across the river and slightly upstream from the small city of St. Louis. This site was chosen in part because it was in the United States — the Louisiana Purchase had not yet been formalized and they did not want to raise any hackles until the land transfer was complete — and also because they didn't want to be too close to St. Louis with its temptations of booze and women while training their men for the rigors of the expedition. They established Camp Wood near present Alton, Illinois, and settled down for a dreary winter of drilling, court-martial proceedings on a frequent basis, equipment and food purchases, and further recruitments of men. Nearly every man in the party was ill sometime during the long winter, usually with respiratory ailments from the cold, windy, and humid climate where the Missouri meets the Mississippi.

But finally the spring of 1804 arrived, and with a detachment of Army men and some short-term employees taken on specifically to bring the keelboat back from the Mandan villages in present North Dakota the following year, the party cast off and headed slowly, painfully, up the swift and treacherous Missouri River for the great unknown.

Wood River, Illinois

"The Country about the Mouth of Missouri is pleasent rich and partially Settled On the East Side of the Mississippi a leavel rich bottom extends back about 3 miles, and rises by several elevations to the high Country, which is thinly timbered with Oakes..." (Clark at Wood River, No date)

Tavern Cave on the Missouri River at St. Albans, Missouri

... we passed a large Cave on the Lbd. Side (Called by the french the Tavern —
about 120 feet wide 40 feet Deep & 20 feet high   many different immages are
Painted on the Rock at this place ..." (Clark, May 23, 1804)

Wild plum and deciduous forest on Missouri River in Missouri

Sunset on the Missouri River at Council Bluffs, Iowa

"The Prarie which is situated below our Camp is above the high water leavel and rich covered with Grass from 5 to 8 feet high interspersed with copse of Hazel, Plumbs, Currents (like those of the U.S.) Rasberries & Grapes . . ." (Clark. August 1, 1804)

The passing of Sergeant Floyd: Wild rose on the Missouri River in Iowa

"... at the first Bluff on the S.S. Serj. Floyd Died with a great deal of Composure ... We buried him on the top of the bluff 1/2 Mile below a Small river to which we Gave his name ... This Man at all times gave us proofs of his firmness and Determined resolution to doe Service to his Countrey and honor to himself ..." (Clark, August 20, 1804)

Spirit mound at Vermillion, South Dakota

Bison on the move

"Capt. Clark killed ... 2 buffaloe, I also killed one buffaloe which proved to be the best meat ... we saved the best meat, and from the cow I killed we saved the necessary materials for making what our wrighthand cook Charbono, calls boudin blanc, and immediately set him about preparing them for supper; this white pudding we all esteem one of the greatest delicacies of the forrest ..." (Lewis, May 9, 1805)

Missouri River and blazing star, Vermillion, South Dakota

"I formed a Camp of the french & the guard on Shore, with one Sentinal on
board of the boat at anchor, a pleasant evening   all things arranged for both Peace
of War, ..." (Clark. October 8, 1804)

Missouri River at Trudeau's Post, South Dakota

Pronghorn

Sioux Indian country: Fort Pierre National Grassland, South Dakota

Teton (Bad) River, Fort Pierre South Dakota

Willow bottoms along the Teton (Bad) River at Fort Pierre, South Dakota

Summer storm over Medicine Creek, Big Bend Gorge, South Dakota

Sioux-Assiniboine camp in North Dakota

Missouri River at Bismarck, North Dakota

Ice jam on the frozen Missouri River at Washburn, North Dakota

Winter at the confluence of the Missouri and Knife Rivers, North Dakota

Mandan lodges at Fort Lincoln State Park, Mandan, North Dakota

"the situation of our boat and perogues is now allarming, they are firmly inclosed in the Ice and almost covered with snow — the ice which incloses them lyes in several stratas of unequal thicknesses which are seperated by streams of water . . . as soon as we cut through the first strata of ice the water rushes up and rises as high as the upper surface of the ice and thus creates such a debth of water as it renders it impracticable to cut away the lower strata . . ." (Lewis, February 3, 1805)

From St. Louis to Fort Mandan

It was raining and blowing that Monday, May 14, 1804, and the departure for the Missouri River was held up until about four o'clock in the afternoon. The party was anxious to be off, but not so anxious that they were willing to take a chance on being swamped in the choppy Mississippi. When they finally did leave, they rowed and towed and pushed for two days before arriving at the French village of St. Charles on the Missouri River, then sat for five more frustrating days waiting for Lewis to come from St. Louis with the last odds and ends of equipment.

This last-minute delay contributed further to the morale problem that plagued the expedition during the long winter. The incidence of fighting and insubordination increased, now that they were in civilization. The men got drunk at dances given in their honor, and one of the perpetual problems, John Collins, received fifty lashes for his behavior at a ball and for saying unkind things to Clark afterward. William Werner and Hugh Hall went AWOL and got twenty-five lashes each. The list of misdemeanors in St. Charles grew quite lengthy.

Finally, on Monday, May 21, they were ready to go. Their roster showed three sergeants; Charles Floyd, John Ordway and Nathaniel H. Prior, and at least 25 privates: William E. Bratton, John Collins, John Colter, Pierre Cruzatte, George Drouillard, Joseph Field, Reuben Field, Patrick Gass, George Gibson, Silas Goodrich, Hugh Hall, Thomas P. Howard, Francois Labiche, Hugh McNeal, John Newman, John Potts, Moses B. Reed, George Shannon, John Shields, John B. Thompson, William Werner, Joseph Whitehouse, Alexander H. Willard, Richard Windsor, and Peter M. Wiser.

Also included was the boat crew assigned to return the keelboat the following spring from the Mandan villages, led by Corporal Richard Warfington. As we shall see, some were later dropped from the expedition and others added on the Lower Missouri, making it virtually impossible to draw up an accurate roster of the trip to Mandan. Beyond there, the roster was complete and easy to follow, and the crew a functioning unit, unlike the first stretch and its shakedown aspects.

When they got under way for the unknown, many must have wondered at the wisdom of joining the expedition while they traversed what was to become the state of Missouri. The river there offered the widest range of agony of any stretch, even the portages and sharp stones in Montana. There was enough game to give them excellent food, perhaps the only pleasant thing about those first few weeks. The current ran from four to five miles an hour and was marked by bluffs that forced the men into the water while towing the keelboat with long ropes. The river had sandbars, low islands, swift and narrow channels, banks that caved in when the men stood on them, sawyers (trees imbedded in the bottom), that swung back and forth to entangle or upend the boats, tree branches drifting into the ropes, sudden thunderstorms with high winds and flashing lightning . . . all this made the trip memorable for its misery.

And that wasn't all. They cut their feet on the bottom, and stumbled over rocks and logs hidden beneath the muddy water. They kept the commanders busy with their limited medical knowledge and primitive first-aid kits by complaining of boils, abscesses, sore feet, bunions, sunstrokes, dysentery, colds, fevers, callouses, snakebites, headaches, colic, rheumatism, sore throats, and toothaches. These ailments were treated with a variety of proven medical discoveries, including poultices, potions, and bleeding.

The captains could do little about slithering snakes, ticks, gnats, and the scourge of North America's wildernesses, mosquitos. Some were almost as large as house flies and they flew in thick swarms, clogging the men's noses, eyes and ears, and flung themselves into their food with abandon. The men carried pieces of tree branches or weeds to brush them away, made smoky fires, coated their exposed flesh with bear grease, and whenever possible, crept beneath netting brought along for that purpose. On those days when there was no breeze to keep them away, they must have had yearned to join the dog Scannon in his agonized howling.

This stretch of the trip was also the major breaking-in period, and Lewis and Clark continued having problems with discipline, particularly with Collins and Hall. In late June they assigned Collins to guard the whiskey barrel, the proverbial fox guarding chickens. He got drunk on the whiskey and shared his booty with Hall. Collins got 100 lashes and Hall fifty. A few days later Willard fell asleep on guard duty and he received 100 lashes.

In spite of the multitude of problems, a routine evolved rapidly that remained in effect throughout the expedition. Two and sometimes three men were assigned to be hunters, usually led by the superior woodsman Drouillard. The Field brothers, Reuben and Joseph, were often with him as was the young George Shannon. Frequently Lewis went with them not only to hunt, but also to observe the surrounding countryside. He was more at ease on a horse or walking, while Clark was an experienced boatman who enjoyed the company of the crew. Lewis was a more introspective man, perhaps even a loner, and Clark was outgoing and even-tempered, a good companion who enjoyed the company of others.

The cooks prepared only two meals a day, and no midday cooking was done. Whenever possible, which was most of the time during the early stage of the journey, they did not dip into their larder of salted meat but lived off the land. They had enough fresh meat to make jerky to supplement the permanent food supply and carry for the midday meal. During the first month the hunters killed at least 70 deer, more than a dozen black bear, three turkeys, a rabbit, a woodchuck, and a goose.

In spite of the painful river conditions, they were able to average about 14 miles a day on the Lower Missouri, which meant that sometimes they went only four or five miles, and other days covered nearly thirty miles. While the men were busy rowing, poling and towing the boats, Lewis and Clark were busy following Jefferson's orders. Lewis made voluminous notes of flora and fauna encountered along the riverbank, and Clark made the celestial observations, drew the maps and kept a journal that complemented Lewis's. Both were excellent observers of the passing scene.

Lewis: "this specimine is the seed of the Cottonwood which is so abundant in this country . . . this tree arrives at a great size, grows extreemly quick the wood is of a white colour, soft spungey and light, perogues are most usually made of these trees, the wood is not durable nor do I know any other valuable purpose which it can answer except that just mentioned."

Clark: "Set out early   great appearance of wind and rain   (I have observed that Thunder & lightning is not as common in this Countrey as it is in the atlantic States) Snakes are not plenty, one was killed to day large and resembling the rattle Snake, only something lighter . . . In every bend the banks are falling in from the current being thrown against those bends by the Sand points which inlarges and the Soil i believe from unquestionable appearns of the entire Bottom from one hill to the other being the Mud or Ooze of the river at Some former Period mixed with Sand and Clay easily melts and Slips into the River and the mud mixes with the water and the Sand and is washed down and lodges on the points."

It is obvious that Lewis had the better education, as befits the secretary to the President of the United States. But Clark, in spite of wild and erratic spelling and endless sentences, was his equal in dispensing information that would be useful to the President, as well as to scholars for centuries to come.

By the end of July the party had traveled through the dense woodlands of Missouri and swung almost due north where the Missouri takes a big bend between Missouri and Kansas. Here the timber thinned considerably and the first indications of the Great Plains made themselves known. They began seeing animals prevalent in the plains, such as badgers and elk. Apparently the badger *(taxidea taxus)* was the first specimen killed to be sent back to the seat of learning on the East Coast, and it also was Lewis's first attempt at his new-found art of taxidermy.

They killed their first buffalo in present South Dakota, near Vermillion, and it was Joseph Fields who had the honor of killing it. Lewis and Sergeant Ordway went with a group of ten men to butcher and bring its meat back to the river, and Ordway commented that " . . . this was the first I ever Saw & as great a curiosity to me."

But before the buffalo was added to their pantry, tragedy struck the expedition. Sergeant Floyd was a favorite among the men as well as the leaders, and on July 31 he wrote in his journal that "I am verry sick and has ben for Sometime but have Recovered my helth again." But by August 18, he was severely ill again. The whole day had been a mixture of the pleasant and the unpleasant. First, Drouillard had been sent out with Reuben Field, Bratton, and Labiche to track down two deserters, Reed and La Liberte. They returned with only Reed because La Liberte escaped them. Reed was court martialed that day, found guilty, and punished on the spot. He was forced to run the gauntlet four times between two rows of the men as they flogged his bare back. Then he was discharged from the expedition and assigned to menial jobs for the rest of the journey to the Mandan villages, where he would remain until the following spring and return to St. Louis with the Army detachment on the keelboat.

August 18 was also Captain Lewis's birthday, and after the punishment of Reed, the men had a celebration in Lewis's honor and were issued an extra ration of whiskey. They sipped and danced to the tune of Cruzatte's fiddle far into the night.

But Sergeant Floyd was mortally ill. By the following morning it was apparent the medicine chest held no cure for him, and at noon they pulled to shore at the southern end of what is now Sioux City, Iowa, to prepare a bath for him. But before they had a chance to, he whispered, "I am going away," and died, the first member of the American Army to die west of the Mississippi, and the only member of the Lewis and Clark expedition to lose his life.

His fatal ailment has since been diagnosed as peritonitis from an infected or ruptured appendix. No doctor alive at that time could have saved him because the first appendectomy was not performed until near the end of that century.

They buried him atop a high hill, then continued on their journey with Patrick Gass selected by the enlisted men to replace Floyd.

Through this section of the river they held frequent councils with Indian tribes, which gave them an opportunity to make anthropological notes while delivering the Great White Father sermon. These councils were always marked by the expedition's concern for peaceful negotiations and the giving of gifts, including a special peace medal struck by President Jefferson for the expedition. Many of these medals were handed down through generations of Indian leaders and have been returned to museums across the country.

But when they reached the mouth of the Teton (Bad) River at present Pierre, South Dakota, the Teton Sioux there were not so easily impressed with the newcomers. The Indians first stole the last horse the expedition owned, then started harrassing the party and at one point appeared to have Clark trapped alone onshore. But this tense moment was ended quickly by a show of force from the men on the keelboat, and Indian leaders stopped other efforts to start a fight with the explorers.

They continued on upriver with a brief stopover to visit the Arikara Indians in north-central South Dakota, an agricultural people who apparently had been driven out of their original land in Oklahoma and Kansas years earlier. But the visit was brief. It was October and the nights were getting colder, water was freezing in pots and shallow depressions, and migratory waterfowl had been flying south for some weeks. The explorers were anxious to reach the Mandan villages and get their winter quarters built. They finally arrived on October 26, about sixty miles upstream from Bismarck, and by their calculations, 1,600 miles from Camp Wood. After several days of scouting for a good location, they selected one six miles downstream from the Mandan villages and started building a small fort. With two facing rows of connected cabins and a high palisade of poles behind it, and a semi-circular palisade around the front with a low gate cut into the middle.

Fort Mandan was completed on Christmas Day, 1803, and they settled down to the long winter of constantly hunting food, making clothing and tools, trading iron weapons and tools made by Shields on the small forge for corn and other food products grown by the Indians, and putting their notes, specimens, and observations in order to send east that spring.

It was also at this winter stop where they picked up three more members of the expedition: Toussaint Charbonneau, his teen-aged wife — a Shoshoni he had bought named Sacajawea — and their infant son born that winter, Jean Baptiste. History has been flatteirng to Sacajawea but not so kind to her husband, who appears to have been lazy and a chronic complainer who also was less than kind to his wife and child. He was hired on as an interpreter, the only task he appears to have been reasonably good at.

So they sat out the long winter, working with the Indians and studying their culture, always searching for food, often giving medical treatment to ill Indians and simply surviving the cold and waiting for the spring thaw so they could be on their way.

Spring greens in the Badlands of North Dakota, Theodore Roosevelt Memorial Park, North Dakota

Rock outpost on the Little Missouri River, North Dakota

"Several Indians came to see us this evening, amongst others the Sun of the late
Great Chief of the Mandins (mourning for his father), this man has his two little
fingers off; on inquireing the cause, was told it was customary for this nation to
Show their greaf by some testimony of pain, and that it was not uncommon for them
to take off 2 Smaller fingers of the hand (at the 2d joints) and some times more with
other marks of Savage effection . . ." (Clark. October 25, 1804)

Badlands of North Dakota

*"Coal or carbonated wood pumice stone lava and other mineral apearances still
continue. the coal appears to be of better quality; I exposed a specimen of it to the
fire and found that it birnt tolerably well, it afforded but little flame or smoke, but
produced a hot and lasting fire." (Lewis: April 22, 1805)*

Clay erosion forms along the Missouri River near Wolf Point, Montana

"I could not discover the junction of the rivers immediately, they being concealed by the wood; however, sensible that it could not be distant I determined to encamp on the bank of the Yellow-stone river which made it's appearance about 2 miles South of me." (Lewis. April 25, 1805)

Yellowstone River upstream from the confluence with the Missouri River near Cartwright, North Dakota

Sandstone concretions at the confluence of the Missouri and Milk Rivers near Fort Peck, Montana

"the country appears much more pleasant and fertile than that we have passed for several days; the hills are lower, the bottoms wider, and better stocked with timber, which consists principally of cottonwood, not however of large size ..." (Lewis. May 1, 1805)

Balsam root blooms

"The wind continued violent all night nor did it abate much of its violence this morning, when at daylight it was attended with snow which continued to fall untill about 10 A. M. being about one inch deep, it formed a singular contrast with the vegitation which was considerably advanced." (Lewis. May 2, 1805)

Cottonwood bottoms in the Charles M. Russell National Wildlife Refuge, Montana

"... here the river ... is filled with a number of small and handsome Islands covered with cottonwood   some timber also in the bottoms, the land again fertile. these appearances were quite reviving after the drairy country through which we had been passing ..." (Lewis, May 28, 1805)

Approaching storm over the Missouri River, Charles M. Russell Wildlife Refuge, Montana

Missouri River above the Mussellshell confluence, Charles M. Russell National Wildlife Refuge, Montana

Bearpaw Mountains above the Judith River, Montana

"Our medisons, Instruments, merchandize, clothes provisions &c&c which was nearly all wet we had put out to air and dry, the day being cloudy & rainey those articles dried but little to day. our hunters killed several deer & saw three Bear one of which they wounded." (Clark. May 15, 1805)

Judith River upstream from the confluence with the Missouri River

Missouri River, Charles M. Russell Wildlife Refuge, Montana

Black Butte and storm, Judith River, Montana

Castles and mushrooms in the Missouri Breaks, Montana

"Set out at an early hour and proceeded principally by the toe line, using the oars mearly to pass the river in order to take advantage of the shores. scarcely any bottoms to the river; the hills high and juting in on both sides, to the river in many places. the stone tumbleing from these clifts and brought down by the rivulets . . . became more troublesome today." (Lewis. May 26, 1805)

Cap rock in the Missouri Breaks, Montana

Moonrise over the Missouri Breaks, Montana

"The hills and river Clifts which we passed today exhibit a most romantic appearance. The bluffs of the river rise to a hight of from 2 to 300 feet and in most places nearly perpendicular ..." (Lewis. May 31, 1805)

Concretions at Eagle Creek in the Missouri Breaks, Montana

"These walls pass the river in several places, rising from the water's edge much
above the sandstone bluffs which they seem to penetrate; thence continuing their
course on a streight line on either side of the river through the gradually ascending
plains, over which they tower to the hight of from ten to seventy feet untill they reach
the hills, which they finally enter and conceal themselves." (Lewis. May 31, 1805)

Evening primrose and yucca, Montana

Confluence of the Marias and Missouri Rivers at Loma, Montana

"to mistake the stream at this period of the season, two months of the traveling season having now elapsed, and to ascend such stream to the rocky Mountain or perhaps much further before we could inform ourselves whether it did approach the Columbia or not, and then be obliged to return and take the other stream would not only loose us the whole of this season but would probably so dishearten the party that it might defeat the expedition altogether." *(Lewis. June 3, 1805)*

Evening storm at Great Falls, Montana

Great Falls of the Missouri River, Great Falls, Montana

"after wrighting this imperfect discription I again viewed the falls and was so much disgusted with the imperfect idea which it conveyed of the scene that I determined to draw my pen across it and begin agin, but then reflected that I could not perhaps succeed better than pening the first impressions of the mind ..." (Lewis. June 13, 1805)

Missouri River and Rocky Mountains at Craig, Montana

"the water decends in one even and uninterupted sheet to the bottom wher dashing against the rocky bottom rises into foaming billows of great hight and rappidly glides away, hising flashing and sparkling as it departs . . ." (Lewis, June 14, 1805)

Limestone cave above Meriwethers Canyon in Helena National Forest, Montana

Gates of the Mountains, Missouri River, Montana

"it was late in the evening before I entered this place and was obliged to continue
my rout untill sometime after dark before I found a place sufficiently large to encamp
my small party; at length such an one occurred on the lard. side where we found
plenty of lightwood ... from the singular appearance of this place I called it the
gates of the rocky mountains." (Lewis. July 19, 1805)

Missouri River, Townsend, Montana

Bull elk

Prickly pear cactus and The Beaverhead, Twin Bridges, Montana

60   *Beaverhead River and prickly pears in bloom, Twin Bridges, Montana*

Limestone arch above the Gallatin River, Three Forks, Montana

"...supposing this to be the three forks of the Missouri I halted the party on the
Lard. shore for breakfast. and walked up to the S. E. fork about 1/2 a mile and
ascended the point of a high limestone clift..." (Lewis. July 27, 1805)

Giant wild rye along the Jefferson River at Silver Star, Montana

Lemhi Pass in the Bitterroot Range on the Idaho-Montana border

Detail of Agency Creek on the west side of Lemhi Pass, Idaho-Montana border

"after refreshing ourselves we proceeded on to the top of the dividing ridge from which I discovered immence ranges of high mountains still to the West of us with their tops partially covered with snow. I now decended the mountain about 3/4 of a mile which I found much steeper than on the opposite side, to a handsome bold runing Creek of cold Clear water. here I first tasted the water of the great Columbia River." (Lewis. August 12, 1805)

Spear point

Red Butte and Shoshone Cove on Horse Prairie Creek, Montana

Salmon River below North Fork, Idaho

"*The River from the place I left my party to this Creek is almost one continued rapid, five verry considerable rapids the passage of either with Canoes is entirely impossible, as the water is Confined between huge Rocks & the Current beeting from one against another for Some distance below . . .*" (Clark. August 23, 1805)

Salmon River near Tower Creek, Idaho

"Capt. Lewis set out this morning very early and poroceeded but slowly ... along
the steep side of a mountain over large irregular and broken masses of rocks ... now
perfectly satisfyed as to the impracticality of this rout either by land or water ..."
(Lewis. August 23, 1805)

The Towers in the Bitterroot Range, Idaho

"This day we passed over emence hils and Some of the worst roads that ever horses passed, our horses frequently fell   Snow about 2 inches deep when it began to rain which termonated in a Sleet." (Clark. September 3, 1805)

September snow on Lost Trail Pass, Montana-Idaho border

"Several horses Sliped and roled down Steep hills which hurt them verry much the one which Carried my desk & Small trunk Turned over & roled down a mountain for 40 yards & lodged against a tree, broke the Desk the horse escaped and appeared but little hurt   Some others verry much hurt . . ." (Clark: September 15, 1805)

Rock slide in Lost Trail Pass, Bitterroot Range, Idaho

Trapper Peak in Bitterroot Range, Montana

Travelers Rest, Lolo Creek and Bitterroot River, Lolo, Montana

"we continued our rout down the valley about 4 miles and crossed the river; it is
hear a handsome stream about 100 yards wide and affords a considerable quantity
of very clear water, the banks are low and it's bed entirely gravel . . . we called this
Creek Travellers rest." (Lewis. September 9, 1805)

Glade Creek camp in Packer Meadow, Bitterroot Range, Idaho

"... *we proceeded over a mountain to the head of the Creek which we left to our
left and at 6 miles from the place I nooned it, we fell on a Small Creek from the left
which Passed through open glades* ..." *(Clark. September 13, 1805)*

Falls along Lolo Creek, Bitterroot Range, Idaho

Lochsa (Kooskooskee) River at Colt-killed Creek, Powell Ranger Station, Idaho

Wendover Creek on lower approach to Lolo Trail, Clearwater National Forest, Idaho

Upper Wendover Ridge winterscape, Bitterroot Range, Lolo Trail, Idaho

*"I have been wet and as cold in every part as I ever was in my life, indeed I was
at one time fearfull my feet would freeze in the thin Mockiesons which I wore . . ."
(Clark. September 16, 1805)*

Bitterroot Range along Lolo Trail, Idaho

Small prairie along Eldorado Creek near Weippe, Idaho

Upper Hungry Creek, Lolo Trail, Idaho

Clearwater River near Orofino, Idaho

"The Saddles were buried on the Side of a bend about 1/2 mile below. all the
Canoes finished this evening ready to be put into the water. I am taken verry unwell
with a pain in the bowels & Stomach, which is certainly the effects of my diet which
last all night." (Clark. October 6, 1805)

Snake River Canyon near Clarkston, Washington

"The Countery thro' which we passed to day is Similar to that of yesterday open
plain no timber   passed several houses evacuated at established fishing places ..."
(Clark. October 13, 1805)

Rapids on the Tucannon River, Washington

"...the water is confined in a Chanel of about 20 yards between rugid rocks for the distance of a mile and a half, and a rapid rockey chanel for 2 miles above. This must be a verry bad place in high water, here is great fishing place..." (Clark. October 13, 1805)

Moss design along Snake River, Washington

Turning sumac in Snake River Canyon, Washington

"A cool morning, deturmined to run the rapids, put our Indian guide in front
our Small Canoe next and the other four following each other, the canoes all passed
over Safe except the rear Canoe which run fast on a rock at the lower part of the
Rapids ..." (Clark. October 16, 1805)

Palouse River near confluence with Snake River, Washington

Captain's Rocks on Columbia River near Wallula, Washington

Arrow and spear point

Miller Island in Columbia River Narrows, Celilo, Washington

Cascade on the Palouse River, Washington

The Dalles, Columbia River, Oregon-Washington

"we thought if necessary to lay in a Store of Provisions for our voyage and the fish being out of Season, we purchased forty dogs for which we gave articles of little value, such as bells, thimbles, knitting pins, brass wire and a few beeds . . ." (Clark. October 18, 1805)

Fog-shrouded St. Peter's Dome, Columbia River Gorge, Oregon

"... *we proceeded on down   the water fine, rocks in every derection for a fiew miles*
when the river widens and becoms a butifull jentle Stream of about half a mile wide
..." (Clark. October 25, 1805)

Mt. Hood, Cascade Range, Oregon

"(from this rapid the Conical mountain is S.W. which the Indians inform me is not far to the left of the great falls; this I call the Timm or falls mountain it is high and the top is covered with snow) (Clark. October 21, 1805)

Beacon Rock State Park, Washington, from Oregon side of Columbia River

Pictograph ("She Who Watches Over"), Horsethief State Park, Washington

"gave this great chief a Medal and some other articles, of which he was much pleased. Peter Crusat played on the violin and the men danced which delighted the nativs, who Shew every civility towards us. we Smoked with those people untill late at night, when every one retired to rest." (Clark. October 25, 1805)

Maple turning along Columbia River, Washington

Ellowa Falls, Columbia River Gorge, Oregon

Storm over Crown Point, Columbia River, Oregon

Naselle River basin, Willapa Wildlife Refuge, Washington coast

Cape Disappointment, Pacific Ocean, Washington

"rained all the last night without intermition, and this morning. wind blows verry hard, but our situation is Such that we cannot tell from what point it comes. one of our canoes is much broken by the waves dashing it against the rocks. 5 Indians came up in a canoe, thro' the waves, which is verry high and role with great fury."
(Clark. November 14, 1805)

From Fort Mandan to the Pacific

From Fort Mandan on was land never seen before by a white man, and the explorers anxiously paced the banks of the Missouri in the early spring of 1805 waiting for the ice to clear so they could press onward. During the winter they had several conferences with the Indians about the river beyond, and from them they received very accurate descriptions and crude maps of what to expect. It was thus they heard of the Great Falls of the Missouri and the portage it entailed. The only information they received that was garbled involved the true Missouri at one crucial point: where the Marias River and the Missouri intersected. They were to spend several precious days camped at this point trying to decide which stream to follow, and finally chose the proper one by instinct and hunch.

When the ice cleared from the river, the keelboat and crew departed for St. Louis on April 7, and simultaneously the 32-member Corps of Discovery headed upstream in the opposite direction, paddling six new cottonwood dugouts and the two pirogues brought all the way from Pittsburgh. They were ready, as Lewis wrote in some of his most memorable words:

"This little fleet altho' not quite so rispectable as those of Columbus or Capt. Cook, were still viewed by us with as much pleasure as those deservedly famed adventurers ever beheld theirs; and I dare say with quite as much anxiety for their safety and preservation. we were now about to penetrate a country at least two thousand miles in width, on which the foot of civilized man had never trodden; the good or evil it had in store for us was for experiment yet to determine, and these little vessels contained every article by which we were to expect to subsist or defend ourselves. however, as the state of mind in which we are, generally gives the colouring to events, when the immagination is suffered to wander into futurity, the picture which now presented itself to me was a most pleasing one . . . The party are in excellent health and sperets, zealously attached to the enterprise, and anxious to proceed; not a whisper of murmur or discontent to be heard among them, but all act in unison, and with the most perfict harmony."

The first few weeks of the renewed journey went by with no problems, and conditions were idyllic compared with most of the upriver journey the previous year. They no longer had to haul the keelboat against the swift current, and the men worked well together paddling and sailing the vessels. Food was everywhere along the banks and hunters could kill all the meat they required without losing sight of the river. They saw no Indians, and wouldn't see any until the following autumn, when they desperately needed them.

But in the sixth week of their paddling, on May 14, to be exact, they had a bad day indeed. First, they learned that the Indians' fear of grizzlies was well founded. They had killed one on April 29 with no trouble, and the explorers took a dim view of the Indians' attitude toward them. But six men were out hunting and found a grizzly lying on the open ground near the river. Four of the men opened fire on him, and all hit the mark. The bear ignored the wounds and charged. The other two men shot then, and one bullet broke the bear's shoulder. But he kept coming. They prudently ran for their lives. But the wounded bear, in spite of the shattered shoulder and two bullets in his lungs, overtook them at the river bank. Two men jumped into a canoe and started paddling furiously and the other four hid in some willows and reloaded, then began firing again. The bear took the shots again and almost caught two men before they dove off a twenty-foot bank into the river. The bear followed and almost had one of the men when a marksman on the bank put a bullet in the bear's brain. When they dressed him out they found eight bullets in him. Nobody again doubted the Indians' reasons for steering clear of the giant animal.

On that same day, toward the end of the day's paddling, Charbonneau ("the most timid waterman in the world" according to Lewis) was in a pirogue well offshore that contained the explorers' papers, books, instruments, and trade goods. A sudden windstorm hit and turned the boat so that the square sail was flat to the wind. It almost went over, and tilted far enough for some of the papers to float away as water rushed over the gunwale.

Cruzatte, blind in one eye and near-sighted in the other, but nonetheless an excellent boatman, told Charbonneau to grasp the rudder and pull the boat around into the wind or he would shoot him. Charbonneau believed him and did as he was told. In the meantime, Sacajawea endeared herself to the whole crew by calmly holding her baby, by now called Little Pomp, with one hand and plucking paper out of the river with the other.

Now they were in some of the most spectacular scenery in the West, perhaps the most beautiful anywhere along the course of the Missouri. This is the area called the Missouri Breaks, a 180-mile stretch of river that winds through white sandstone cliffs, one of the few sections of the river still much the same as the explorers saw it.

The Missouri Breaks occupied only about four days of the explorers' trip, but it was four days of neck-craning and superlatives from the pens of the captains. On May 31, Lewis made a try at describing what they saw during the day:

"The hills and river Clifts which we passed today exhibit a most romantic appearance. The bluffs of the river rise to the hight of from 2 to 300 feet and in most places nearly perpendicular; they are formed of remarkable white sandstone which is sufficiently soft to give way readily to the impression of water; two or three thin horizontal stratas of white freestone, on which the rains or water make no impression, lie imbeded in these clifts of soft stone near the upper part of them; the earth on the top of these Clifts is a dark rich loam, which forming a gradualy ascending plain extends back from ½ mile to a mile where the hills commence and rise abruptly to a hight of about 300 feet or more. The water in the course of time in decending from those hills and plains on either side of the river has trickled down the soft sand clifts and woarn it into a thousand grotesque figures, which with the help of a little imagination and an oblique view, at a distance are made to represent eligant ranges of lofty freestone buildings, having their parapets well stocked with statuary; collumns of various sculpture both grooved and plain, are also seen supporting long galleries in front of those buildings; in other places on a much nearer approach and with the help of less immagination we see the remains or ruins of eligant buildings; some collumns standing and almost entire with their pedestals and capitals; others retaining their pedestals but deprived by time or accident of their capitals, some lying prostrate an broken othe[r]s in the form of vast pyramids on their tops becoming less as they ascend and finally terminating in a sharp point. nitches and alcoves of various forms and sizes are seen at different hights as we pass . . ."

Lewis wrote on for several pages describing and attempting to explain this spectacular landscape, a remarkable performance in both descriptive and scientific writing. It is landscape to haunt one's memory for years to come.

The crossing of the Great Falls portage was one of the hardest jobs they faced, and they came to hate those falls even though when they first saw them they were as enchanted as inlanders the first time they look upon the ocean.

During the preparations for the portage, and the portage itself, Sacajawea lay in her tent more dead than alive with a stomach ailment, delirious and, as Lewis wrote, "with strong nervous symptoms, that of the twitching of the fingers and leaders of the arm." They treated her with poultices of bark and fed her great quantities of mineral water from a nearby spring, and before the day ended, she was feeling much better.

They decided what they needed for the rest of the journey, then dug jug-shaped holes in the ground near the river to cache the remainder of their gear. The largest of the pirogues also was hidden because it was too heavy for the portage. Then they chopped down cottonwood trees, cut sections and made crude wheels for rough wagons to haul the boats and gear over the seventeen-mile portage. The portage began on June 21 and was completed on July 2, during which time the explorers were in constant agony from the prickly pears and sharp rocks that cut through their deer and elkskin moccasins.

But, in the words often used in their journals, they proceeded on upriver, through the stunning and sheer cliffs they called Gates of the Mountains just north of Helena, Montana, then south to the three rivers that form the Missouri: The Madison, Gallatin and Jefferson, all named by the explorers. Now they were in the high valley where they hoped to find Sacajawea's people, the Shoshoni, and buy horses. Even though it was July, they were concerned about getting over the mountains and down the Columbia to the ocean before winter.

After several days of struggling up the meandering, shallow Jefferson River, towing the canoes and the remaining pirogue, Sacajawea put herself into the history books and the explorers' hearts by recognizing landmarks along the route from her childhood before she was stolen by raiding Indians and sold into slavery. Then, in one of those incidents almost too contrived for novelists and screenwriters, when they finally did make contact with the Shoshoni, none other than her own brother was the chief! Lewis and Clark got their horses.

From the Shoshoni encampment near Lemhi Pass on to the Pacific, the explorers traveled as fast as they dared. They had two rather inept Indian guides take them north along the unnavigable Salmon River and over Lost Trail Pass from present Idaho back into Montana to a flat meadow they called Traveler's Rest. From there they struck out west again over Lolo Pass in the Bitterroot Mountains and down into Weippe Prairie. The crossing was made with extreme difficulty. Snow was still deep, game was almost nonexistent and they had to kill some of the horses for meat. Pack horses fell often, damaging or destroying equipment. When they arrived in the valley near present Orofino, Idaho, they were so starved that when they first ate meat, they became very ill. Some were sick for several days on the salmon offered by the gracious Nez Perce Indians along the Clearwater River.

They remained no longer than absolutely necessary and set to work building canoes, left their horses with the Nez Perce and paddled off down the Clearwater and into the treacherous Snake River in southeast Washington before the men were completely healthy. They shot the rapids with less trouble than expected, had only occasional capsizings, and at last entered the broad Columbia River.

By now it was October, and when they left the barren, sun-bleached desert east of the Cascade Range and entered the damp and overcast Columbia Gorge, they knew winter would catch them before they reached the ocean. They were plagued by unfriendly Indians along the river, who had already had contact with white traders on the Lower Columbia. The honesty and integrity of the Shoshoni, the Mandans, and the Nez Perce were almost totally lacking among these Columbia River Indians. And to compound the difficult situation, they were attacked by ferocious fleas in the campsites along the river, making it necessary to travel totally nude much of the time.

The Columbia River at that time was a test for boatmen, and they had to make frequent portages around the worst of the rapids and line the canoes through from the steep, treacherous banks. But they survived this set of problems, too, and entered the broad, calm Lower Columbia in mid-October. By early November they were near enough to the ocean to be conscious of the tides that sweep up and down the river, and on November 10, they were at journey's end. The weather was miserable: rain and fog and wind that did not let up for weeks at a time.

They landed first on the Washington side of the Columbia estuary but could not find a suitable place for a camp that would be their home for several months. There wasn't sufficient game on the northern shore, and they did not trust the Chinook Indians who lived there. After scouting both sides of the river for several days, Lewis found a good site up a small river on the southern side of the Columbia where there were abundant trees for the fort and firewood, and signs of deer and elk for food and clothing.

They began building the fort in early December, naming it Fort Clatsop in honor of the local Indians who were helpful, and were moved in by Christmas Eve.

Although the temperature seldom dropped near freezing that winter, the almost constant rain and overcast skies made life as miserable for the men as Fort Mandan had been. Their clothing was never dry, and frequently disintegrated from the dampness, and they suffered from various colds and bronchial problems. But

Lewis and Clark kept very busy with their reports and transcribing notes into comprehensible form for future readers.

They did not always have enough to eat because the elk and deer moved farther and farther away from the fort during the winter. Often their meat was, in their terminology, "pore." We would call it rotten today. But they kept hunters out day after day and they had to travel farther and farther away from camp for game, sometimes two or three days' travel.

There were many other activities to keep them occupied. The leaders, of course, kept busy with their writing and produced some of the most thorough, and sometimes humorous, anthropological comments of the trip. The local Indians had been exposed for several years to white traders who traveled the coast, and they not only were more adept at trading but also were more nimble-fingered when they saw something they wanted. The Indians also had a working knowledge of prostitution and the leaders had to lock up everything of value to keep the men from trading them for the women's "favors." But the Clatsops were not warlike, and diplomatic relations went along smoothly through the winter.

Large quantities of salt were needed for both cooking and preserving food, and after searching the beach from the mouth of the Columbia southward, they established a salt-making works on a sandspit with trees for shelter several miles south, at the site of Seaside, Oregon. There men were assigned on a revolving basis, and their main chores were keeping a fire burning beneath large pots in which seawater was boiled away, leaving the salt crusted in the pots.

Then a few days after New Year's Day, 1806, two of the saltmakers returned to Fort Clatsop with the news a whale had washed up on shore south a few miles from the salt works, and the Indians were carving it up. The two men, Willard and Wiser, brought along a chunk of the blubber and the leaders decided they should make an expedition down to see what this was all about.

Clark decided to lead the group of 11 men, but Sacajawea pleaded to go along because she had come all this way and still hadn't seen the ocean. Clark, always a soft touch for Sacajawea and her son, agreed and Charbonneau decided to accompany them. They left on January, 6, killed an elk and ate it while camped overnight on the trail to the salt works. They arrived there the next morning and Clark hired a local Indian to lead them over the high headland, now called Tillamook Head, and down to the beach where the whale's carcass lay. He paid the Indian "a file in hand and promised Several other small articles on my return." They struck out down the beach and "proceeded on the round Slipery Stones under a high hill which projected into the ocean about four miles further than the direction of the Coast. After walking for 2½ miles on the Stones, my guide made a Sudin halt, pointed to the top of the mountain and uttered the word *Pe shack* which means bad, and made signs that we could not proceed any further on the rocks, but must pass over that mountain . . . and after about 2 hours labour and fatigue we reached the top of this high mountain, from the top of which I looked down with estonishment to behold the hight which we had assended, which appeared to be 10 or 12 hundred feet up a mountain which appeared to be almose perpindicular . . . "

Alas, the trip was almost wasted because the Indians had carved away nearly all the meat and blubber, but Clark was able to purchase about 300 pounds and a few gallons of whale oil. One of the men, McNeal, was lured into a lodge by an Indian man and woman for sexual purposes, he thought, but actually they meant to kill him. A Clatsop woman they knew from around the fort began screaming and the Indian couple left McNeal intact.

It was while with these Indians that Clark made one of the most hilarious entries into his journal, the famous smoking entry:

"The Clatsops Chinnooks and others inhabiting the coast and country in this neighbourhood, are excessively fond of smoking tobacco. in the act of smoking they appear to swallow it as they draw it from the pipe, and for many draughts together you will not perceive the smoke which they take from the pipe; in the same manner also they inhale it in their lungs untill they become surcharged with this vapour when they puff it out to a great distance through their nost[r]ils and mouth; I have no doubt the smoke of the tobacco in this manner becomes much more intoxicating and that they do possess themselves of all it's virtues in their fullest extent; they freequently give us sounding proofs of it's creating dismorallity of order in the abdomen, nor are those light matters thought indelicate in either sex, but all take the liberty of obeying the dictates of nature without reserve."

The rest of the winter was largely anticlimactic. They began planning their departure shortly after Christmas, and finally settled on April 1 as the day to begin the return journey. But weather prevented it, and they didn't get off until April 22, after making a gift of Fort Clatsop to the local chief, Comowool, who had been a good friend. At about 1 p.m. that afternoon, beneath a clear sky, they cast off and paddled down to the Columbia, then headed upstream and homeward.

Driftwood and Tillamook Head

"*The wind which is the cause of our delay, does not retard the motions of those people at all, as their canoes are calculated to ride the highest waves, they are built of white cedar or Pine verry light wide in the middle and tapers at each ends, with aperns, and heads of animals carved on the bow, which is generally raised.*" (Clark. October 28, 1805)

Spruce forest and sword fern, Tillamook Head, Ecola State Park, Oregon

Young's River cascade, Clatsop County, Oregon

"... Capt. Lewis returned with 3 men in the Canoe and informs me that he thinks a Sufficient number of Elk may be pr/o/cured convenient to a Situation on a Small river ..." (Clark. December 5, 1805)

Snow frosting on Coast Range, Clatsop County, Oregon

Fort Clatsop, detail

". . . our fortification is completed this evening and at Sun set we let the nativs know that our Custom will be in future, to Shut the gates at Sun Set at which time all Indians must go out of the fort and not return into it untill next morning after Sunrise at which time the gates will be opened . . ." (Clark. December 30, 1805)

Fort Clatsop National Memorial, near Astoria, Oregon

Cascade and alder forest, Coast Range, Oregon

"nothing occured to-day, or more So, than our Wappato being all exhausted."
(Clark. January 4, 1806)

"nothing extraordinary happened today." (Lewis. January 7, 1806)

Haystack Rock, Cannon Beach, Oregon

"*Two of our canoes have been lately injured very much in consequence of the tide leaveing them partially on shore. they split by this means with their own weight.*"
(Clark. March 3, 1806)

Clearing storm off Cannon Beach, from Ecola State Park, Oregon   115

Wet mat of leaves, Clatsop County, Oregon

"The coast in the neighbourhood of Clarks Mountain is slipping off & falling into the Ocean in immence masses; fifty or a hundred acres at a time give way and a great proportion in an instant [is] precipitated into the Ocean." (Lewis. January 10, 1806)

Trillium, Clatsop County, Oregon

Skunk cabbage design, Clatsop County, Oregon

Spring leafing out along Oregon Coast

Multnomah Falls, Oregon

"the most remarkable of these casscades falls . . . perpendicularly over a solid rock
into a narrow bottom of the river on the south side . . ." (Lewis. April 9, 1806)

"these rapids are much worse than they were [in the] fall when we passed them,
at that time there were only three difficult points within seven miles, at present the
whole distance is extreemly difficult of ascent . . ." (Lewis. April 11, 1806)

Oneonta Gorge, Columbia River, Oregon

Snowpack in Bitterroot Range above Weippe, Idaho

Travelers Rest, Lolo Creek, Montana

*"last evening the indians entertained us with setting the fir trees on fire. they have
a great number of dry limbs near their bodies which when Set on fire create a very
sudden and emmence blaize from bottom to top of those tall trees. they are a boutifull
object in this situation at night." (Clark. June 25, 1806)*

Blackfoot country near Ovando, Montana

"... the Minnetares of Fort de prarie and the blackfoot indians rove through this quarter of the country and as they are a vicious lawless and reather an abandoned set of wretches I wish to avoid an interview with them if possible ..." (Lewis. July 17, 1806)

Pine on Lewis and Clark Pass, Montana

Blackfoot outpost on Lewis and Clark Pass, Montana

Great Falls of the Missouri River, Montana

"these falls have abated much of their grandure since I first arrived at them in June 1805, the water being much lower ... I determined to take a second drawing of it in the morning." (Lewis. July 16, 1806)

Giant Springs, Great Falls, Montana

Pompey's Pillar, Yellowstone River, Montana

"this rock I ascended and from it's top had a most extensive view in every direction.
This rock which I shall call Pompy's Tower is 200 feet high and 400 paces in se-
cumpherance and only axcessable on one Side . . ." (Clark. July 25, 1806)

Yellowstone River near Columbus, Montana

"I was much disturbed last night by the noise of the buffalow which were about me. one gang swam the river near our Camp which alarmed me a little for fear of their Crossing our Canoes and Splitting them to pieces. Set out as usial about Sun rise   passed a rapid which I call wolf rapid from the circumstance of one of those animals being at the rapid." *(Clark. July 31, 1806)*

"I was alarmed on the landing of the Canoes to be informed that Capt. Lewis was wounded by an accident. I found him lying in the Perogue, he informed me that his wound was slight ..." *(Clark. August 12, 1806)*

Confluence of Missouri and Yellowstone Rivers, Williston, North Dakota   135

St. Charles, Missouri

"...at 4 PM we arived in Sight of St. Charles, the party rejoiced at the Sight of
this hospota/b/l/e/ village plyed thear ores with great dexterity and we Soon arived
opposit the Town ..." (Clark. September 21, 1806)

From Fort Clatsop through the Journey Home

The problems and frustrations of a long journey through new country are easier to tolerate while the goal is still beyond the horizon, especially if it is a place you've never been before. But the return journey is likely to be a sheer necessity, something one must accept, and one's thoughts are more likely to wander or concentrate on problems back home, or the shortcomings of one's traveling companions.

It was thus for the Lewis and Clark party, although home was still five months of hard travel from Fort Clatsop, a full season between spring thaw and winter freeze. With their orders followed admirably, probably more completely and with more embellishments than Jefferson had hoped for, still the leaders were unsatisfied. It was as though they did not want this trip to end, filled as it was with discomfort and dangers. They had plans for elaborating it once they crossed the Continental Divide. But they first had to cross it, which involved going against the strong current of the Columbia and Snake Rivers, then back over the miserable Lolo Trail.

For the first several days they paddled up the Columbia, hugging the south bank and riding the tidal flow upriver, then sitting out the ebb that today can stop a tug in its own wake. When they reached the first rapids, their progress was slowed even more and it took them ten days to portage around the Cascades, Narrows, and Celilo Falls. To make matters worse, they had more problems with the Indians here than on any other portion of the trip, the trivial but irritating problems of constant theft. The Indians stole everything they could carry away, including Scannon, briefly.

Finally, at present Hood River, Oregon, they took the advice of friendly Indians and decided to depart the river and ride horses over a trail across the barren plains to the Clearwater and the Nez Perce encampment they had left the previous autumn. There they had left several head of horses, and had cached some gear in a pit. They traded as many goods as they could spare and finally collected enough horses and rode along a route south of the Snake River through sagebrush and bunchgrass and were welcomed warmly by the Nez Perce.

For nearly a month they sat in the camp waiting for snow to clear from the Bitterroot Mountains. They waited from May 14 to June 10, irritable and anxious. Tempers flared, and on one occasion an Indian and Lewis almost had a fight. Ridiculing Lewis because the party bought dogs for meat much as one would buy cattle, the Indian threw a small dog in Lewis's lap while he was eating and made some insulting remark about dog eaters. Lewis hurled the poor mongrel back at the Indian and told him he would apply a tomahawk to his skull if it happened again.

Finally, in mid-June they pushed off for Weippe Prairie on the first stage of a battle with the snow drifts. They left the prairie without a guide, but were turned back a few days later by the deep drifts. They sent Drouillard back to the Nez Perce camp to hire guides, and he returned a few days later with three, who agreed to lead them over Lolo Pass in exchange for a rifle each. A week later, on June 30, they were back at Travelers Rest, the mountains behind them.

Here they did a dangerous thing. They split the party into two groups, then each group would later split again. Lewis was to take his group to explore the Marias River because they thought it might be a navigable route into the north country of present Canada. He would send half of his group directly down the Missouri to the Great Falls to dig up the cache and get everything ready for the float down the Missouri. He would meet them at the mouth of the Marias after he finished his exploration.

Clark would take his group back over the Continental Divide to Camp Fortunate, where they had met Sacajawea's people the previous autumn. They would go overland until they hit the Yellowstone River, follow it until it was deep enough to float boats, build them and float down to the river's confluence with the Missouri. Clark was to split his party and send a group led by Sergeant Pryor overland on the horses directly to the Mandan villages. There Pryor was to hire a North West Company trapper named Hugh Heney to persuade some Sioux chiefs to accompany the expedition back to Washington, D.C.

Lewis had the most trouble, and his poor judgment has led some historians to wonder at his mental stability. They went far enough up the Marias to see that it was an insignificant stream, and were preparing to return to the Missouri when they encountered a party of Blackfeet. Although he did not trust them, they shared a camp that night. The following morning the Indians made their move. They attempted to steal the party's guns, and Lewis and his men went on the attack. Lewis shot one in the stomach and Reuben Field stabbed another, killing him. The others fled, and so did Lewis and his men. They made a remarkable ride over the rough, barren country, almost nonstop for more than 100 miles. Almost miraculously, they arrived at the Missouri exactly at the same time as the party from Great Falls.

Lewis's troubles weren't over yet. In his party was Pierre Cruzatte, the boatman-fiddler-cook who was blind in one eye and near-sighted in the other. While hunting in a thicket, Cruzatte mistook Lewis for an elk and shot him in the buttocks. Lewis thought they were being attacked by Indians because Cruzatte was too horrified to answer his cries. Lewis lay on his belly most of the way back to St. Louis.

Clark's trip was less exciting. They got their gear together and went to Three Forks and split into two groups, as planned. Clark went over Bozeman Pass, a route Sacajawea remembered from her childhood, and they followed the Yellowstone several miles before finding timber large enough for dugouts. Pryor took his contingent overland, and on the second night out, their horses were stolen by Crow Indians. They walked on to the sandstone tower Clark had already found and named for Sacajawea's child, "Pompy's Pillar," and inscribed his name on it where it still remains. Pryor and his men killed some buffalo, feasted on the meat and used the hides to build three round Indian-style "bullboats." Then they floated down the Yellowstone behind Lewis, "rub-a-dub-dub, three-men-in-a-tub."

The party was reunited at the confluence of the Yellowstone and Missouri, then drifted together down to the Mandan villages. They spent only three days there, but during that time were able to convince a chief, Sheheke, to accompany them back to Washington, D.C. He took along his wife and young son, and two canoes were lashed together like a catamaran for their comfort.

On August 17, 1806, they were on the last long leg of the journey homeward. They paddled hard, and only stopped to hunt and eat and sleep. On one occasion they bartered with a trader for some whiskey. Then, on September 23, they pulled into St. Louis and found that most people had assumed they were long dead.

They had lost only one man, and Sergeant Floyd undoubtedly would have died no matter where he was when he was stricken. They had killed only two people, and it was a case of clear-cut self-defense, which isn't a bad record for an Army detachment traveling more than two years in strange country. They had opened up the west to Americans. They whetted the appetite for westward expansion to land's end, and told the nation what was between the oceans and how to get there. Perhaps more than any other individuals in our history, they were responsible for America taking its present shape.

One cannot help but wonder what the men thought of the journey after it was completed. We know that some went back West immediately, and some stayed, as did Colter after meeting some trappers on the Yellowstone. Charbonneau and Sacajawea — and "Little Pomp" — stayed in the Mandan villages. We know that while Clark lived a long, healthy, and happy life, Lewis apparently committed suicide a short time later. We know that Clark's slave, York, was given his freedom and enough money to start a freighting business, and we know that Sergeant Gass outlived them all.

But what of the others who drifted into total obscurity? Unfortunately, few people realized the impact the journey had on history until years later, and men who should have been accorded the same honors of a statesman, military hero, or an entertainer, died and were buried as anonymously as most are born. When Clark died, the funeral procession in St. Louis was a mile long. But nobody knows the grave of Pierre Cruzatte, and for that matter, nobody knows for certain the grave of Sacajawea. Nevertheless, history has been kinder to them than to most secondary figures in exploring parties.

BOOKS FOR FURTHER READING

Bakeless, John Edwin *Lewis and Clark, Partners in Discovery,* New York, W. Morrow, 1947.

Burroughs, Raymond D. *The Natural History of the Lewis and Clark Expedition.* Michigan State University Press, East Lansing, 1961.

Chidsey, Donald Barr. *Lewis and Clark: The Great Adventure.* Crown, 1970.

Coues, Eliott, ed. *History of the Expedition Under the Command of Lewis and Clark.* Dover Publishing Co., New York, 1965 (reprinted from the 1895 edition).

Criswell, Elijah Harry. *Lewis and Clark: Linguistic Pioneers.* University of Missouri Press, Columbia, 1940. o.p.

Cutright, Paul Russell. *Lewis and Clark: Pioneering Naturalists.* University of Illinois Press, Urbana, 1969.

DeVoto, Bernard. *The Course of Empire.* Houghton Mifflin Company, Boston, 1952.

_____. *The Journals of Lewis and Clark.* Houghton Mifflin Company, Boston, 1953.

Eide, Ingvard Henry. *American Odyssey: The Journey of Lewis and Clark.* Rand McNally, 1969.

Lewis, Meriwether, and Clark, William. *History of the Expedition of Captains Lewis and Clark, 1804-5-6.* Introduction and index: James K. Hosmer, McClurg, Chicago, 1924 (reprinted from 1814 edition).

Wheeler, Olin D. *The Trail of Lewis and Clark, 1804-1904.* G.P. Putnam's Sons, New York and London, 1926 o.p.

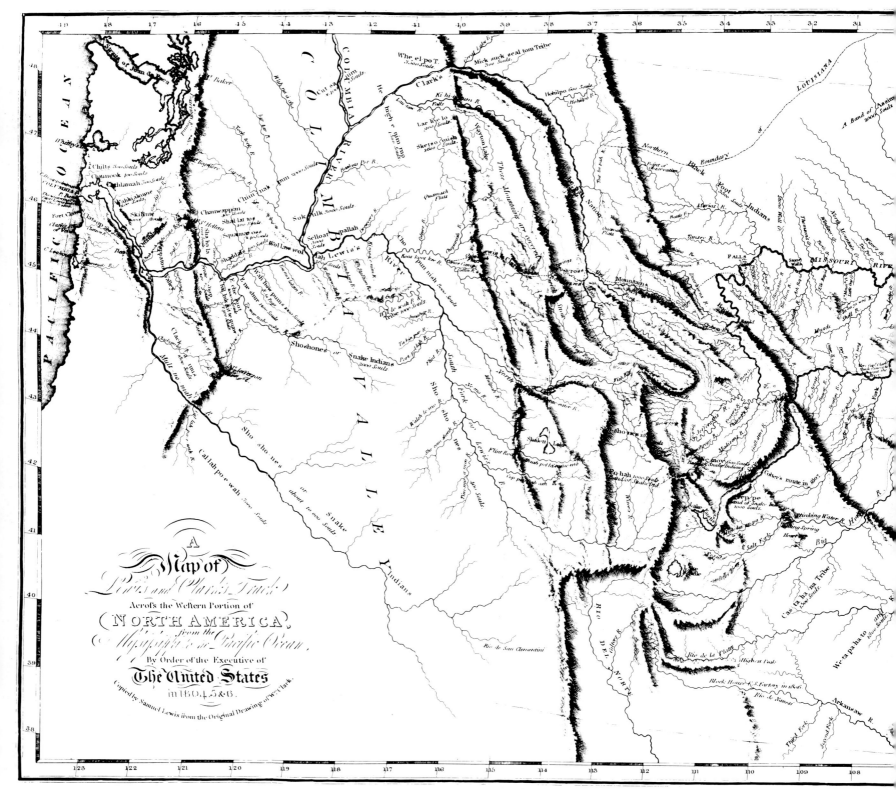

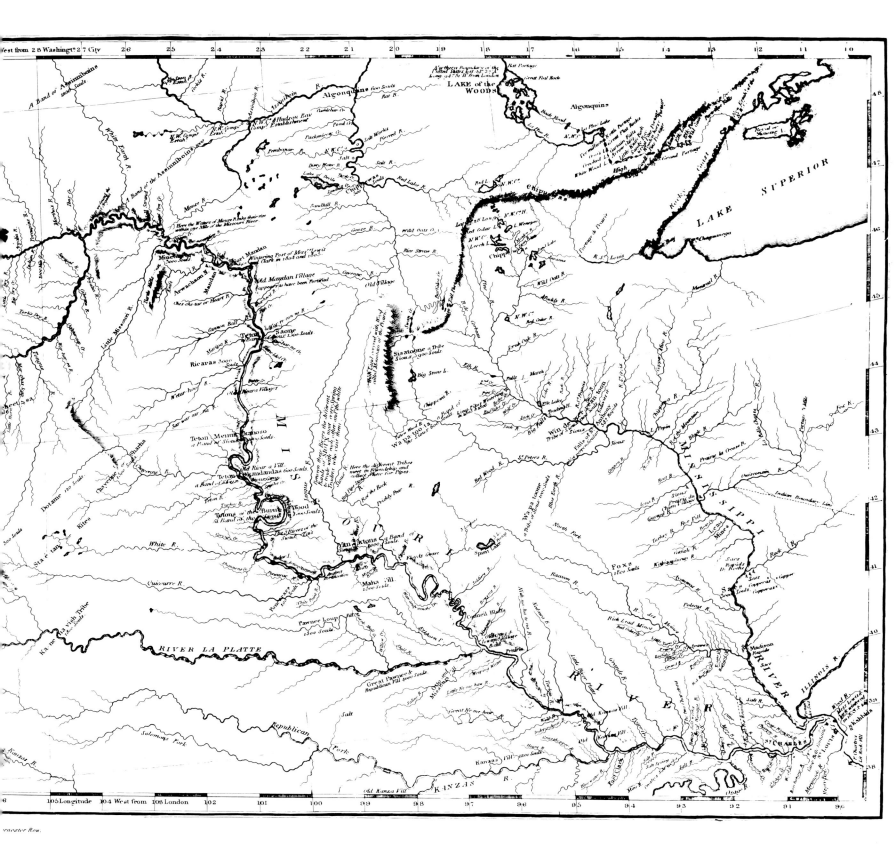

143

ACKNOWLEDGEMENTS

Excerpts from the Lewis and Clark Journals appearing in the text and captions are taken from the Reuben Gold Thwaites edition published by Arno Press, New York, in 1969.

Portions of this book appeared in a different form in *National Wildlife.*

Mr. Satterfield wishes to thank Winnebago, Inc., and Kampgrounds of America (KOA) for assistance while retracing the Lewis and Clark Trail.

Lithography by
Fremont Litho, Inc.
Fremont, California

Color separations by
San Diego Color Service
San Diego, California